Amphibians

Sally Morgan

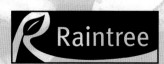
Raintree

www.raintreepublishers.co.uk
Visit our website to find out more information about **Raintree** books.

To order:
 Phone 44 (0) 1865 888113
 Send a fax to 44 (0) 1865 314091
 Visit the Raintree Bookshop at **www.raintreepublishers.co.uk** to browse our catalogue and order online.

 Produced for Raintree by
White-Thomson Publishing Ltd
Bridgewater Business Centre, 210 High Street
Lewes, East Sussex, BN7 2NH

First published in Great Britain by Raintree,
Halley Court, Jordan Hill, Oxford OX2 8EJ,
part of Harcourt Education.
Raintree is a registered trademark of Harcourt Education Ltd.

© Harcourt Education Ltd 2005
The moral right of the proprietor has been asserted.

Consultant: Dr Rod Preston-Mafham
Editorial: Katie Orchard, Nick Hunter and Catherine Clarke
Design: Tim Mayer
Picture Research: Sally Morgan
Production: Amanda Meaden

Originated by Dot Gradations Ltd
Printe in China by WKT Company Limited

ISBN 1 844 43773 6
09 08 07 06 05
10 9 8 7 6 5 4 3 2 1

British Library Cataloguing in Publication Data
Morgan, Sally
Amphibians. – (Animal Kingdom).
597.8
A full catalogue record for this book is available from the British Library.

Acknowledgements
The publishers would like to thank the following for permission to reproduce photographs: Corbis pp.9 bottom (Joe McDonald), 21 top and 25 top (Chris Mattison/Frank Lane); Digital Vision Title page, contents page, pp.4, 6, 18, 36, 42, 44 bottom, 45, 46, 48; Ecoscene pp. 31 top (Kjell Sandved), 33 (John Pitcher), 38 (Anthony Cooper), 40 (R.A. Beatty), 43 (Anthony Cooper); Ecoscene/Papilio pp.7 top, 10 top and 11 (Robert Pickett), 15 top (Paul Franklin), 15 bottom (David Manning), 17 top (Robert Pickett), 19 top and 24 (Jamie Harron), 26–27 and 27 top (Paul Franklin), 37 bottom (Robert Pickett), 41 bottom (Paul Franklin); Nature pp.8 (Fabio Liverani), 9 top (Phil Savoie), 10 bottom (Reijo Jurrinen), 13 (Mark Payne Gill), 17 bottom (Ingo Arndt), 23 bottom (Barry Mansell), 26 top (Fabio Liverani), 28 (Morley Read), 32 top (John Downer Productions), 39 top (Jose B Ruiz), 41 top (George McCarthy), 44 top (John Cancalosi); NHPA pp.5 top (T. Kitchin and V. Hurst), 7 bottom (Daniel Heuclin), 12 top (ANT), 12 bottom (Nobert Wu), 14 (Stephen Dalton), 16 (Kevin Schafer), 18 bottom (Daniel Heuclin), 20 (Stephen Dalton), 21 bottom (Kevin Schafer), 22 (Robert Erwin), 23 top, 25 bottom and 29 top (Daniel Heuclin), 28 bottom (Jenny Sauvanet), 30 (Daniel Heuclin), 32 bottom (Stephen Dalton), 34 (Pierre Petit), 35 top (Anthony Bannister), 35 bottom (Daniel Heuclin), 36 top (James Carmichael), 39 bottom (Bill Coster); Photodisc pp.5 bottom, 31 bottom.

Cover photograph of strawberry poison frogs reproduced with the permission of NHPA (T. Kitchin and V. Hurst).

Every effort has been made to contact copyright holders of any material reproduced in this book. Any omissions will be rectified in subsequent printings if notice is given to the publishers.

The paper used to print this book comes from sustainable resources.

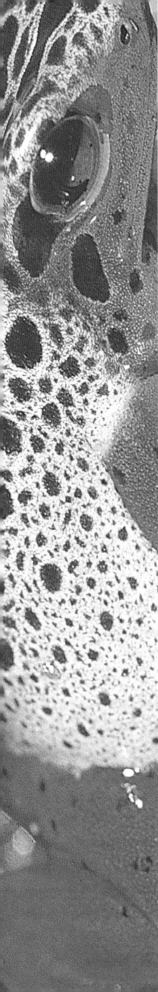

Contents

Any words appearing in the text in bold, **like this**, are explained in the Glossary.

Introducing amphibians

Frogs, toads, salamanders and newts are all **amphibians**. The word 'amphibian' means an animal that lives part of its life on land and part in water. This is true for most amphibians, but there are some that spend their entire lives in water or on land.

Amphibians belong to a large group of animals called **vertebrates**. These are animals with backbones. Other vertebrates include fish, **reptiles**, birds and **mammals**.

Breathing

Although most amphibians have lungs, many rely on their skin to breathe and hardly ever use their lungs. These amphibians have a smooth, moist skin, which allows the passage of oxygen into the body.

▼ All amphibians, including this ornate horned toad, undergo metamorphosis.

Classification key

KINGDOM	Animalia
PHYLUM	Chordata
SUB-PHYLUM	Vertebrata
CLASS	**Amphibia**
ORDERS	3 – Caudata, Gymnophiona, Anura
FAMILIES	44
SPECIES	5565 and increasing

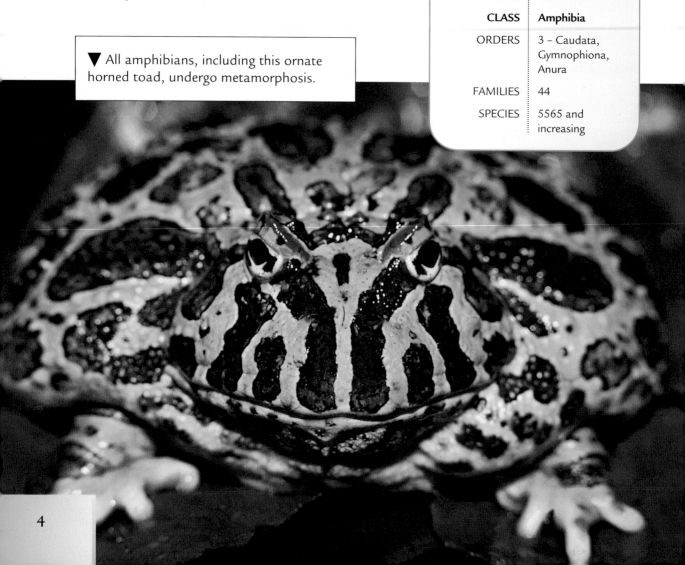

Cold-blooded animals

Amphibians are **ectothermic**, or cold-blooded. This means that their body temperature is similar to the temperature of the environment around them. If the external temperature falls, their body temperature falls, too. At low temperatures amphibians cannot produce enough body heat to stay active, so they become **dormant**, or inactive, until temperatures begin to rise.

Metamorphosis

One of the most important features of amphibians is the fact that they undergo a change in appearance, called **metamorphosis**. The frog, for example, starts life as a **tadpole**.

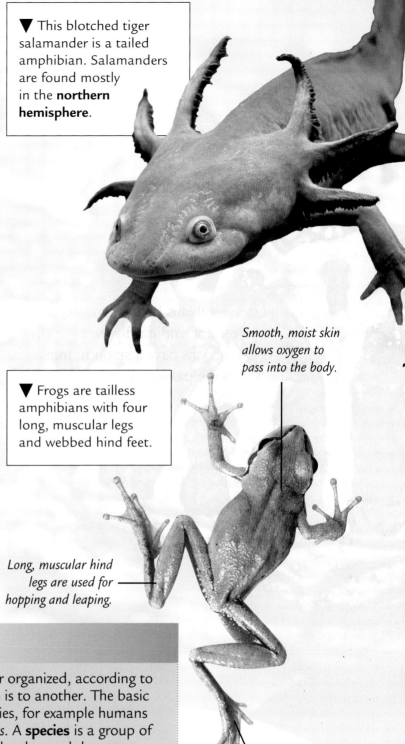

▼ This blotched tiger salamander is a tailed amphibian. Salamanders are found mostly in the **northern hemisphere**.

Smooth, moist skin allows oxygen to pass into the body.

▼ Frogs are tailless amphibians with four long, muscular legs and webbed hind feet.

Long, muscular hind legs are used for hopping and leaping.

Webbed hind feet propel the frog easily through water.

Classification

Living **organisms** are classified, or organized, according to how closely related one organism is to another. The basic group in classification is the species, for example humans belong to the species *Homo sapiens*. A **species** is a group of individuals that are similar to each other and that can **interbreed** with one another. Species are grouped together into genera (singular: genus). A genus may contain a number of species that share some features. *Homo* is the human genus. Genera are grouped together in families, the families grouped into orders and the orders grouped into classes. Amphibians are in the class Amphibia. Classes are grouped together in phyla (singular: phylum) and finally the phyla are grouped into kingdoms. Kingdoms are the largest groups. Amphibians belong to the animal kingdom. (To find out more see pages 42–43.)

Amphibians are found in freshwater habitats on every continent except Antarctica. They cannot live in salt water. Most live near water as they have to return to water in order to **breed**. However, many salamanders live a completely **terrestrial** life and lay their eggs on land.

Moist skin

Amphibians have smooth, thin skin with no scales or hairs. They can breathe through their skin, absorbing oxygen either from air or water. For this to happen the skin must be kept moist at all times. Amphibians produce **mucus** over their skin that makes it moist and slippery to the touch. Although amphibians have lungs, they breathe mostly through their skin. They use their lungs when they are active and need more oxygen. In water, adult amphibians come up to the surface of the water to take air into their lungs.

Larval amphibians (those at an early stage of development such as **tadpoles**) breathe with **gills**. Gills have a large **surface area** in contact with the water, which means that more oxygen can be picked up by the blood flowing through them. In a young tadpole, the gills are outside the body, but as the tadpole becomes older the gills are covered over. Eventually they are replaced by lungs. These older larvae rely mostly on their lungs to obtain oxygen, although a small amount of oxygen will pass through the skin. Some amphibians that live in water permanently, such as the axolotl, breathe mostly through their gills.

▼ This tinkered frog has a smooth skin, which must be kept moist to allow oxygen to enter its body.

▲ When toads rest at the surface, their eyes lie above the water, allowing them to watch out for predators.

Moving around

Animals that live in water need to be able to swim. Adult frogs and toads, for example, have long legs with webbed feet, which push them through the water. However, on land frogs can use their powerful legs for crawling, hopping and leaping. Newts have a long tail with a fin, which they use to swim and steer. The eyes of a frog have a vertical pupil. This allows the frog to see above the surface of water while keeping the rest of its body under water.

▶ Newts, such as this palmate newt, are found in water during the breeding season. They obtain their oxygen mostly through their skin and mouth.

Life cycle

Amphibians are the only vertebrates to undergo metamorphosis, or a complete change in their appearance.

Egg laying

In most amphibian species the female lays her eggs in water and they are fertilized by the males. The eggs may be laid singly or in batches. The batches of eggs may form long chains or clusters. Amphibian eggs are different from those of reptiles and birds, because they are not protected by a shell. Each egg is made up of a small black spot surrounded by a jelly coating. The black spot is the fertilized egg: a tiny embryo with a much larger yolk sac beneath it. The embryo has all the food it needs in the yolk sac. Some salamanders live on land and do not return to water to breed. They lay a small number of large eggs and the larvae develop inside the eggs before hatching as miniature adults.

Larval amphibians

The embryo grows inside the egg, gradually getting larger and more elongated in shape. The jelly starts to break down and the egg hatches. A newly hatched amphibian is called a larva, or, in the case of frogs and toads, a tadpole. The larvae feed constantly. Often the first food they eat is the remains of the jelly.

◀ Toads, such as these green toads, lay their eggs in long chains, which they wrap around underwater plants so they do not drift away.

▲ This glass frog is guarding her **clutch** of eggs, which she has laid on a leaf.

The tadpoles of frogs and toads and the larvae of newts feed on plants, either filtering their food from the water or scraping off plant material. After a few weeks, they change their diet and become **carnivorous**. Salamander larvae are often **predatory**. As the larvae grow they begin to undergo a gradual metamorphosis, becoming more like an adult. For example, frog and toad tadpoles grow legs and their tail disappears. The larvae of newts and salamanders already look like the adult, so they do not have to undergo such a dramatic metamorphosis. The shape of the tail fin changes and their skin becomes thicker.

Viviparous salamanders

A few salamanders do not lay any eggs. Instead the eggs are kept inside the body of the female. The embryos develop within the eggs, using **nutrients** supplied by the female. The female gives birth to a small number of well-developed larvae. This is called **vivipary**, or live bearing.

Amazing facts

- Fire salamanders are viviparous. The faster-growing young of fire salamanders may eat their smaller siblings while still inside their mother's body.

- The tadpoles of the Surinam horned toad are very aggressive. They are carnivorous from the moment they hatch, and will attack tadpoles of other species and even each other.

▲ This female Jefferson salamander has laid a large clutch of eggs. The eggs will hatch into larvae.

The common frog

In early spring, common frogs (*Rana temporalis*) travel to ponds to **breed**. They often gather in large numbers. Each female lays her eggs, which are then **fertilized** by the males.

Frogspawn

The female frog lays a **clutch**, or cluster, of about 100–200 eggs. The clusters are known as **frogspawn**. Each newly laid egg consists of a blob of protective jelly surrounding a black dot. The black dot is the **embryo** that grows into a **tadpole**. The cells that form the embryo divide and increase in number. Soon the blob becomes longer and it is possible to make out a tiny tadpole. After about ten days, the protective jelly turns to liquid so the tadpole can move around. It wiggles its way out of the jelly and into the water.

Tadpoles

The young tadpoles are **herbivores**, or plant eaters. They feed on pondweed and microscopic **algae** in the water. The tadpoles grow quickly and their long tail helps them to swim around the pond.

▲ At first tadpoles have only a head and a tail. The legs appear later.

▼ Male and female frogs gather in the breeding ponds in early spring.

Each tadpole has tiny external **gills** on either side of the head. They use these gills to breathe by taking in oxygen from the water. These external gills become smaller and, after four weeks, they disappear completely. They are replaced by internal gills, which are protected on the outside by a flap of skin.

Two small bulges appear at the back of the body, either side of the tail. The bulges develop into legs, each of which ends in a webbed foot. The front legs appear a few weeks later. The diet of the tadpole changes from plants to small animals in the water.

There are internal changes, too. The lungs begin to grow and they gradually take over from the internal gills. When this happens, the tadpoles come to the surface of the water to take gulps of air.

Final changes

Finally, the shape of the tadpole changes. The tail becomes shorter until just a stump remains. The backbone becomes more obvious. The round mouth of the tadpole changes to the much wider mouth of the frog and the eyes stick out more. The complete **metamorphosis** takes about twelve weeks. The tiny **froglets** leave the water and live on land for the next few years until they are fully grown and ready to breed.

Classification key	
CLASS	Amphibia
ORDER	Anura
FAMILY	Ranidae
GENUS	*Rana*
SPECIES	***Rana temporalis***

▲ Once a tadpole has developed its front legs, the tail becomes shorter and shorter, and the froglet can leave the water.

Amazing fact

- The paradoxical frog gets its strange name (the word paradox means absurd or contradictory) from the fact that its tadpoles live for a long time and they grow to four times the length of the adult frog.

Extreme survivors

Most **amphibians** live in damp places and need water to survive. However, some amphibians can be found in extreme environments such as hot deserts or the freezing Arctic.

▲ Burrowing frogs store water in their bladder. This allows them to stay under ground without drying out.

Surviving drought

Deserts are dry places where you would not expect to see any amphibians. The daytime temperatures are high and rain is infrequent. When it does rain, there are heavy downpours. However, a few frogs and toads have **adapted** to this dry habitat. They tend to be active at night when the temperatures are lower. Desert frogs and toads survive long periods of dry weather by burrowing under ground. They produce **mucus**, which they spread over their body. The mucus hardens to stop water escaping. Once it is safely cocooned in mucus, the frog goes into a state of **torpor** (becomes completely inactive). It may stay like this for several months or even years until the rains return.

Desert frogs and toads are able to lose lots of body water. They can also take up water quickly. The spadefoot toad can absorb water simply by sitting on a damp patch of ground. The skin touching the ground is thin and rich in **blood vessels**, and the water is quickly absorbed. Some desert frogs and toads can store water in their body. Water-holding frogs have large, baggy **glands** under their skin, which can swell up with water. As much as half their body weight can be water.

◄ A California newt can survive fire by secreting mucus over its body.

▲ This male bullfrog is digging a channel to allow his tadpoles to escape to a larger pool before they dry out.

Arctic frogs

Amazingly, frogs can be found in the far north at the edge of the Arctic. Here they have to survive long, cold winters. They do this by creeping into a safe place where they go into torpor until the temperatures rise again.

Fire survivors

Fires are common on the grasslands and forests of California. California newts have adapted to this danger. They **secrete** mucus all over their body and this protects them so well that they can walk right through the flames.

Amazing facts

- The crab-eating frog of South-east Asia lives beside slightly salty water, where it is said to feed occasionally on crabs.
- The Aboriginal people of Australia use water-holding frogs as a source of water.
- Pools of water do not last long in deserts so the eggs of the spadefoot toad hatch in three days and the **tadpoles** complete their **metamorphosis** in six to eight days.

Colour

Amphibians display an amazing range of colours, from red and black spots through to vivid blues and greens. The colour of the skin comes from **pigments** in the skin cells.

Colour change

Many amphibians can change the colour of their skin by making the area of pigment larger or smaller. This occurs slowly, taking several minutes. The colour of a frog's skin can alter the amount of heat its body absorbs. Dark colours absorb more heat than light colours. By making their skin lighter, some amphibians can reflect heat away from their body, which allows them to cool down. If they are too cool, they can increase the amount of heat they absorb by making their skin darker.

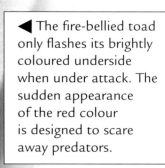

◀ The fire-bellied toad only flashes its brightly coloured underside when under attack. The sudden appearance of the red colour is designed to scare away predators.

▲ This narrow-headed frog is so well camouflaged it can barely be seen against the background tree bark.

Amazing facts

○ To scare off predators, the Italian spectacled salamander raises its tail over its back in a defensive position to reveal the brightly coloured underside of its tail.

○ The Corroboree frog is a vivid yellow with black stripes. The reason for its bright colours is uncertain as it does not produce any poisons from its skin.

Colour for camouflage

Some amphibians use colour to blend in with the background and become **camouflaged**. Some form a pattern of colours that breaks up the outline of the animal so that **predators** cannot see them resting on the ground. Many frogs and toads that live on forest floors look like dead leaves. Some even have a line that looks like the midrib of a leaf running down their back.

Warning colours

Other amphibians are brightly coloured to make them stand out. These are warning colours that tell would-be predators that they are poisonous and should not be eaten, for example, the fire salamander and poison frogs (see pages 36–37). Others use colour to surprise their predators. For example, when attacked the fire-bellied toad flips over and reveals a brightly coloured underside to scare away its attacker. There are some brightly coloured frogs and toads that are not poisonous. They have copied the warning colours of a poisonous **species** to trick predators into avoiding them.

▶ The yellow spots of the fire salamander are a warning that this amphibian **secretes** poisons.

15

Communication

Amphibians make good use of sounds, smells and vision. These senses are important for communication, especially during the breeding season. Many amphibians return to the same pond or stream to breed each year and they use their senses to find their way back. It is thought that they use smells, as well as vision, to find their way.

Vocal sacs

Male frogs often have two types of croak. The main one is rather like an advertisement to tell females that they are waiting. The second croak is more of a territorial or aggressive call, to warn off intruders. The croaking sound of the male frog is produced by vocal cords in the larynx, or voicebox. When the frog breathes out, the air causes the cords to vibrate and produce a sound. At the same time, the frog inflates its vocal sac. Most frogs have a single vocal sac just below the mouth, but some have two sacs, one on each side of the head. The role of the sac is to make the sound louder. The frog may also use its vocal sac to change the sound, to make some sounds louder or to drown out the sounds of other frogs.

◄ These two tree frogs are fighting over territory.

Croaking frogs

A lot of croaking takes place during the breeding season. Sometimes male frogs gather in one place to breed. There is a short period of intense activity when all the frogs croak during a few nights in order to attract the attention of as many females as possible. Because the sound of many frogs croaking is louder than just one frog croaking, each male has a greater chance of finding a female. Some **species** of frogs gather in traditional breeding places, but they do not call at the same time. Each night only a few males will croak. This means that the breeding goes on for a longer period of time, sometimes many months.

Male frogs will also use sound in disputes with other males. When another male comes into their **territory** they will make a sound that is a warning to the other male. If the other male ignores the warning, the males may fight.

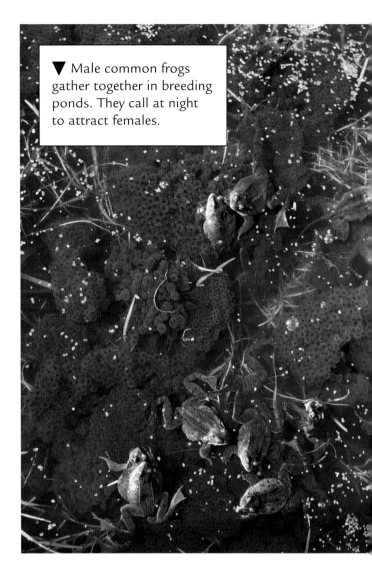

▼ Male common frogs gather together in breeding ponds. They call at night to attract females.

Amazing facts

○ The male Tungara frog calls more than 7000 times in a single night. As well as attracting females, it also attracts bats. The bats swoop down and grab the frogs.

○ Sometimes male frogs make calls to interfere with a neighbouring frog that is trying to attract females!

▼ The natterjack toad has a single vocal sac below its throat, which inflates when it croaks.

Amphibian orders

There are 5565 **amphibian species**, of which 4883 are frogs and toads, 517 are newts and salamanders, and 165 are **caecilians**. Unusually for **vertebrates**, the number of species of amphibians is rising. Since 1985 the total number of recognized species has increased by more than one third and the number is still growing as new species are discovered. However, many species are under threat of **extinction**, so the numbers may start to fall again.

Classifying amphibians

Amphibians are placed in the class of Amphibia. Within this class there are three orders – Anura (frogs and toads), Caudata (newts and salamanders) and Gymnophiona (caecilians).

When classifying amphibians, biologists look at features such as the number of vertebrae, which are the small bones that make up the backbone. For example, salamanders have a long, flexible backbone with many vertebrae, while frogs and toads have a short, strong backbone with far fewer vertebrae. Most amphibians have four limbs. The front limbs have four toes while the hind limbs have five toes. However, some salamanders have either no hind limbs or have fewer toes, and the caecilians are completely limbless. Frogs and toads have much larger heads than the other amphibians. However, most amphibians have well-developed eyes, which they use to find and catch food.

◀ Tree frogs have no tail and they belong to the order Anura.

▲ Tailed amphibians, such as this blue spotted salamander, belong to the order Caudata. They have long bodies and tails.

Fossil amphibians

Amphibians were among the first vertebrates to live on land, more than 300 million years ago. It is thought that they **evolved** from fish that had fleshy front limbs and could flip from pool to pool over land. The earliest **fossil** amphibians are called labyrinthodonts. They were large animals more than 1 metre long that walked very slowly. Most of these early amphibians died out, but two groups survived. One group was Lissamphibia and they became the modern amphibians that we see today. The other group evolved into **reptiles** (see page 45).

Amazing facts

- Miniature salamanders are among the smallest of all vertebrates, being just a few centimetres long. These salamanders have extra-long tongues, more than half the length of the body, which shoot out to catch insects.

- Chinese scientists have discovered Asia's oldest frog fossils, one dating as far back as 125 million years ago.

- The backbone of a frog is made up of approximately twelve bones. A salamander may have as many as 100 bones while a caecilian has up to 250.

▲ The marbled newt, with its mottled black and green skin, is more brightly coloured than other European newts.

19

Tailed amphibians

Salamanders, newts and their relatives belong to the order Caudata. They are found throughout North America, Europe and parts of Asia, but they are not found in the **southern hemisphere**. They have a long, flexible body and tail with four relatively short but sturdy limbs. Some tailed **amphibians** do not have hind limbs. This order of amphibians is thought to be most similar to the earliest amphibians that have long been **extinct**.

Newts and salamanders look very similar. The term 'salamander' is used to describe a tailed **terrestrial**, or land-dwelling, amphibian. The term 'newt' comes from the Anglo-Saxon word '*efete*' or '*evete*' and it refers to those tailed amphibians that return to water to **breed** each spring. Despite these terms, some salamanders are found in water and newts spend many months on land.

Smooth skin

Newts and salamanders have smooth, flexible skin with no scales. Although they have lungs, these amphibians use their skin to obtain oxygen. This can only happen if their skin is kept moist. This means that the newts and salamanders have to stay in damp or wet habitats, such as bogs, marshes and wetlands.

Some tailed amphibians are completely **aquatic** – they spend their entire lives in water. Many of these aquatic amphibians have kept their external **gills**, which they use to breathe.

▼ The smooth newt spends several months each year in water.

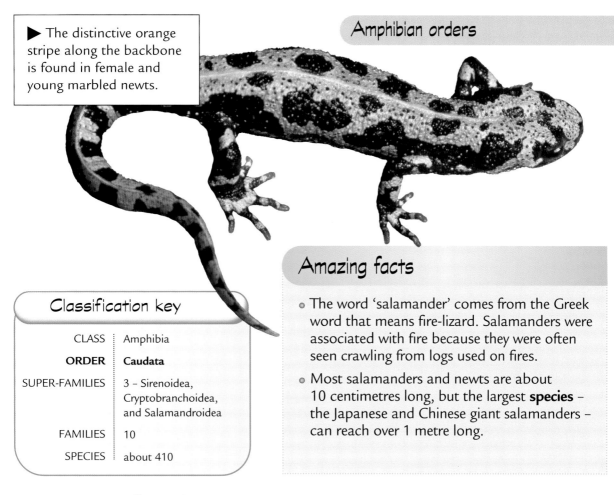

▶ The distinctive orange stripe along the backbone is found in female and young marbled newts.

Classification key

CLASS	Amphibia
ORDER	**Caudata**
SUPER-FAMILIES	3 – Sirenoidea, Cryptobranchoidea, and Salamandroidea
FAMILIES	10
SPECIES	about 410

Amazing facts

- The word 'salamander' comes from the Greek word that means fire-lizard. Salamanders were associated with fire because they were often seen crawling from logs used on fires.

- Most salamanders and newts are about 10 centimetres long, but the largest **species** – the Japanese and Chinese giant salamanders – can reach over 1 metre long.

Life cycle

Not all newts and salamanders have the same life cycle. Some live entirely in water and never go on to land. Others return to water to breed. Their **larvae** live in water while they undergo **metamorphosis**. Some tailed amphibians live only on land and lay eggs that hatch into miniature adults. Others give birth to live young.

▲ The axolotl looks like a giant **tadpole** with external gills. The adults keep their external gills as they are completely aquatic.

Three super-families

Within the order of Caudata there are three **super-families**. The largest is Salamandroidea, which includes newts, European salamanders and mole salamanders. The super-family Sirenoidea contains sirens, and the super-family Cryptobranchoidea contains giant salamanders and Asiatic salamanders.

Sirens and giant salamanders

Sirens and giant salamanders belong to the two **super-families** of Sirenoidea and Cryptobranchoidea (see page 21).

Sirens

There are four **species** of siren and they are only found in some southern states of the USA and northern Mexico. They live in shallow water in ditches, streams and lakes. Sirens are eel-like animals, ranging in length from 10 to 90 centimetres. They spend their entire lives in water. Sirens have external **gills**, which they use to breathe in water. They have a long body with no hind limbs. Their front limbs are small and are found just behind the gills. Their eyes are very small with no eyelids. Sirens are usually brownish-green with pale spots.

All sirens are meat eaters, or **carnivores**, feeding on small animals such as crayfish, worms and snails. A siren feeds by sucking mud, which contains these animals, into its mouth. Unlike most **amphibians**, they do not have teeth at the front of the mouth, but have a horny beak instead. Sirens can survive periods when ditches and ponds dry up by burrowing into the mud and covering themselves in **mucus**, which forms a protective covering, or cocoon, around them. They go into a state of **torpor** (see page 12) and can survive like this for months.

Classification key	
CLASS	Amphibia
ORDER	Caudata
SUPER-FAMILY	**Sirenoidea and Cryptobranchoidea**
FAMILIES	3
SPECIES	42, possibly more

▼ Sirens have a long, eel-like body and external gills.

▼ Hellbenders are North American giant salamanders that have a heavy head and body with four short legs.

Amazing facts

- The greater siren can survive encased in its cocoon for two years without food.
- In Japan giant salamanders are caught and eaten, as they are considered a delicacy.
- One giant salamander in captivity lived to 52 years of age.

Giant salamanders

At 90 centimetres, the giant salamanders are the largest. They live in rivers and streams and are **aquatic**, but unlike the sirens they do not have external gills. They breathe through their skin. There is a fold of skin along the side of their body, which increases the **surface area** through which oxygen can enter the body. They use their lungs, too, and they come to the surface to take gulps of air. Giant salamanders are **nocturnal**, coming out at night to hunt. They eat a variety of animals that they find in the water, including fish, insects and snails.

▼ The Chinese giant salamander lives in fast-flowing mountain streams where the water has plenty of oxygen.

Salamanders and newts

Most tailed **amphibians** belong to the **super-family** Salamandroidea, which includes European salamanders and newts, mole salamanders, olm, mudpuppies, torrent salamanders and lungless salamanders.

Newts

Newts are true amphibians. Adult newts spend up to half the year in water and the rest of the year on land. Their body undergoes a change when they return to the water. Their skin becomes smooth and able to absorb oxygen, their tail becomes more **streamlined** to help them swim and their eyes change shape so that they can focus under water. Some develop webbed feet. When they are in water they can breathe in one of three ways: through their skin, through the lining of the mouth or through their lungs. When they are more active they cannot get enough oxygen through their skin and mouth, so they come up to the surface to take gulps of air. This can be risky because **predators**, such as herons, may spot them.

In spring the mature adults travel to their **breeding** ponds, where they lay eggs in water. Their **larvae** grow rapidly and develop legs. By the end of summer they leave the water looking like small adults. They spend the next few years on land before returning to the ponds to breed.

Classification key	
CLASS	Amphibia
ORDER	Caudata
SUPER-FAMILY	**Salamandroidea**
FAMILIES	7
SPECIES	approximately 370

▼ Newts usually return to the same pond to breed year after year, often travelling several kilometres.

▶ The tiger salamander is one of the most widely distributed of the mole salamanders.

Mudpuppies and waterdogs

These salamanders are totally **aquatic** and they have feathery external **gills** as well as lungs. They live in ponds, lakes and streams. They are predators, feeding on small aquatic animals. The female lays her eggs in spring, sticking each of them to an underwater rock or log. The male guards the eggs until they hatch five to nine weeks later.

Mole salamanders

Mole salamanders are given this name because they live in a burrow for much of their life. They are hardly ever seen except during the breeding season when they travel to ponds to breed. They have a heavy body with smooth, shiny skin that is often brightly coloured. The spotted salamander, for example, is a mole salamander.

▼ The olm has **adapted** to a life in dark caves. It has a long, thin body with a pinkish skin, two pairs of tiny limbs and external gills.

Amazing facts

- California newts have skin **secretions** that are among the most poisonous substances known.
- The spiny newt has long, sharp pointed ribs. If grabbed by a predator, the ribs push out through poison **glands** in the skin.

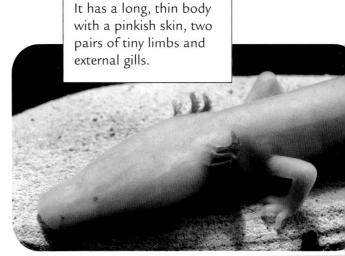

The great crested newt

The great crested newt is a large European newt that spends up to five months of the year in ponds and lakes. The adult male is up to 14 centimetres long. Its orange or yellow underside with black blotches warns **predators** that these newts are poisonous.

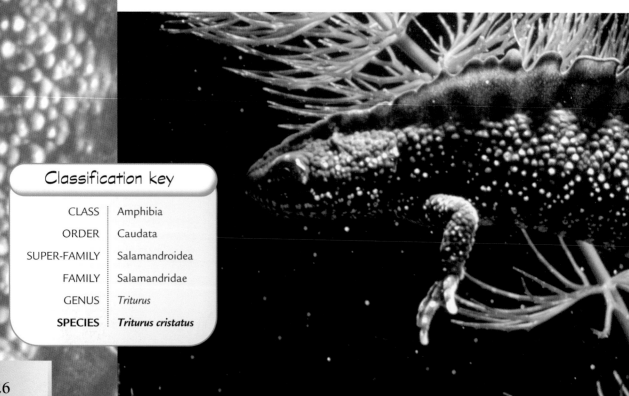

▲ Great crested newts are able to breed when they are about two to three years old.

Habitat

Great crested newts need several different types of habitat during their lives. They spend much of the year on land and can be found in woodlands, scrub and grassland, where they feed on earthworms, insects, spiders and slugs. They are **nocturnal**, hiding on land during the day in burrows or under logs, stones and vegetation. They become inactive between October and late February, when they shelter under piles of leaves or logs, or inside hollow tree stumps and stone walls.

Breeding colours

In early spring, the newts become active again and travel to their **breeding** ponds. This is often the pond in which they were born.

Classification key

CLASS	Amphibia
ORDER	Caudata
SUPER-FAMILY	Salamandroidea
FAMILY	Salamandridae
GENUS	*Triturus*
SPECIES	***Triturus cristatus***

The males undergo an impressive change in appearance when they develop their breeding colours. They have a large, jagged crest along the length of the back, a blue-white streak down the side of the tail and the orange underside becomes more obvious. Females do not have a crest, and they have a yellow-orange stripe along the underside of their tails.

▲ Newt larvae have well-developed tails and external **gills**.

Courtship and change

The newts undergo a complicated courtship. A male swims near a female with his crest standing up. He may nudge the female with his nose and swim around her. Egg laying lasts from March to mid-July. Although each female lays about 200–300 eggs, she only lays two or three eggs per day. These are carefully wrapped in the leaves of **aquatic** plants. The **larvae** hatch after about three weeks. Larval newts usually feed on **tadpoles**, worms, insects and insect larvae. Their **metamorphosis** into air-breathing youngsters takes about four months. At this stage they are ready to leave the pond and live in damp habitats near water.

Amazing facts

- Great crested newts can live for 27 years, possibly more.
- Females choose their **mate** according to the size of the crest.

◀ The adult great crested newt hunts in ponds for other newts, tadpoles, young **froglets**, worms, insect larvae and water snails. They also hunt on land for insects, worms and other **invertebrates**.

Caecilians

Caecilians have a long body without any legs or tail. These **amphibians** are unusual and also the least studied because they spend so much time in burrows. Caecilians are found mostly in Central and South America, southern China, west Africa and parts of South-east Asia.

▼ This South American caecilian has body rings called annuli.

Bodies for burrowing

Caecilians are **adapted** to burrowing. They have a fat and elongated body, which looks as if it is made up of lots of segments, like an earthworm, but this is only an illusion. In fact, their skin is joined to the bones underneath so it does not get ripped off or damaged during burrowing. Caecilians burrow by using their head like a spade. For this reason, their skull is particularly large, heavy and bony. Their eyes are small as they spend most of their time under ground and do not rely on their sight. Land-dwelling caecilians burrow into soil, while the **aquatic species** burrow into mud under water. They move through the ground by contracting (tightening) the muscles in their body. As the muscles contract, they squeeze the fluid inside the body, making the body get longer and move forwards. One unusual feature of the caecilians is the presence of a small tentacle below each eye. The tentacle detects chemicals and is used to find **prey**.

▼ This caecilian is eating a worm. The body of the caecilian looks very similar to that of the worm.

- Caecilians range in size from just 7 centimetres long to 1.6 metres.
- Aquatic caecilians look like eels. They have a fin on their tail, which they use to swim.
- Linnaeus' caecilian has a rear end covered in a hard shield. It also has up to 300 grooves in its skin and within each groove the skin is covered in tiny scales.

Waiting for food

Caecilians are **carnivores**, and feed on earthworms, termites and other animals they find while they are burrowing through the soil. Sometimes they emerge from their burrow and wait for prey to pass close by. This way they may catch lizards, grasshoppers and crickets. However, while they are outside the burrow **predators**, such as snakes and birds, may catch them.

Live birth

Most caecilians are **viviparous** and give birth to live young. Sometimes the young are kept within the female's body for as long as eleven months. A few caecilians lay their eggs in burrows near streams. After they hatch, the tiny **larvae** wriggle into the water. Egg-laying caecilians look after their eggs, guarding them from predators until they hatch.

▼ A few caecilians are aquatic and spend their lives in water.

Classification key

SUB-CLASS	Amphibia
ORDER	**Gymnophiona**
FAMILIES	6
SPECIES	176

Frogs and toads

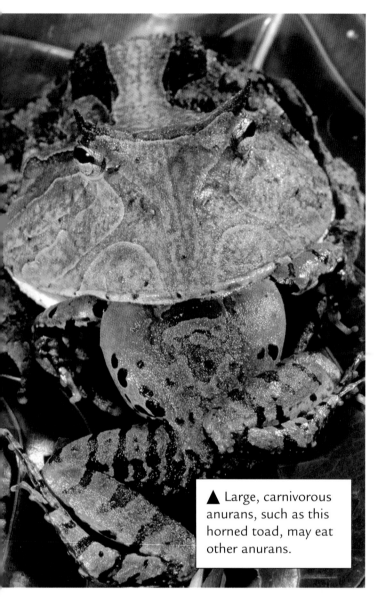

▲ Large, carnivorous anurans, such as this horned toad, may eat other anurans.

Frogs and toads make up most of the **amphibians**. They belong to the order Anura. Frogs and toads are found in a range of habitats from rainforests to mountain slopes. They are most common in the warmer parts of the world, especially the **tropics**, but they can be found as far north as the Arctic. They spend part of the year in water and part on land.

Anuran features

Adult frogs and toads can be distinguished from other amphibians because they have long hind limbs and no tail. The backbone is much shorter than in other amphibians. It is a stiff rod, which gives support when the frog or toad is jumping and landing. Frogs and toads do not have a neck so they cannot move their head from side to side. Most of the time they breathe through their skin and the lining of their mouth. When they are active in water they rise to the surface to gulp air into their lungs.

Amazing facts

○ The African clawed toad has a line of white 'stitch' marks along its sides. These contain sense organs that allow the toad to detect vibrations made by prey or **predators** in the water.

○ The marine or cane toad is the world's largest toad at 24 centimetres long. When threatened it squirts poison into the eyes of its attacker.

▲ Anurans that spend a lot of time in water, such as the African clawed toad, have webbed hind feet like this one.

Feeding

Frogs and toads are **carnivores** and they make good use of their senses, especially their sight, to find their **prey**. They catch prey using their long tongue. Their tongue is only attached at the front of the mouth and this allows the frog or toad to flip out its tongue quickly to catch food. The upper surface is very sticky and can trap prey. A wide mouth allows them to swallow large prey. Some of the larger frogs will tackle prey such as rats and snakes. To swallow, a frog or toad closes its mouth and eyelids and presses down on the food with its eyeballs.

Frog or toad?

Many people describe toads as having a drier, warty skin, and being heavier and slower moving than frogs. In reality there is no difference. Strictly speaking the term 'toad' should only be used for the members of the genus *Bufo*, for example, the common toad *Bufo bufo*. The African clawed toad, *Xenopus laevis*, lives in water, has a smooth skin and is a frog, not a toad.

▼ Frogs and toads have large, bulging eyes with eyelids to protect them from dust and soil. The eardrum can be seen on the side of the head.

Classification key

CLASS	Amphibia
ORDER	**Anura**
FAMILIES	28
SPECIES	approximately 4750

In or out of water?

Frogs that spend a lot of their time in water, for example the edible frog and the bullfrog, have a very smooth skin and a **streamlined** body. Their hind limbs are long and muscular and they end in webbed feet. These features help them move through water with ease. They go on to land, but they rarely travel very far from the water. When threatened by **predators** they leap quickly back into the water.

▲ Wallace's flying frog glides between trees using its huge webbed feet like wings.

Frogs and toads that spend more of their time on land, such as the European toad, have a slightly different shaped body. Their head and body are more rounded, their hind limbs are short and they do not have webbed toes. They may have quite dry skin.

Jumping

The long legs of the frog allow it to push off from the ground with force and to cover a long distance in one go. It lands on its front limbs, which cushion the impact. Frogs tend to hop over the ground rather than make long leaps. A leap is a long jump that is many times the frog's body length. Frogs tend to leap only when they are threatened by predators and need to escape quickly.

▼ To leap, a frog quickly unfolds its hind legs to produce a force that propels it forwards.

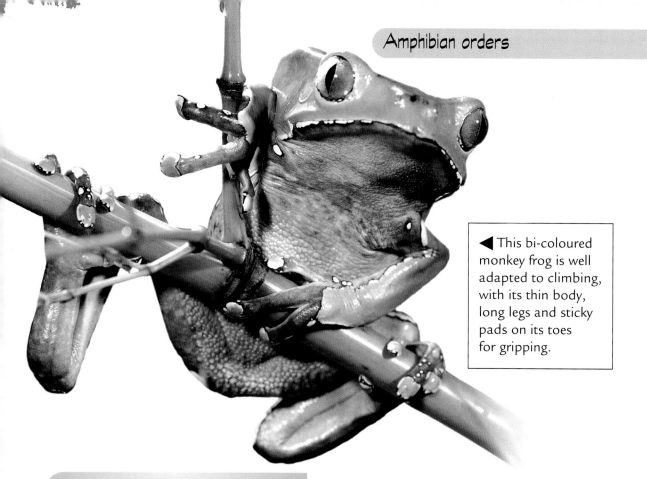

◄ This bi-coloured monkey frog is well adapted to climbing, with its thin body, long legs and sticky pads on its toes for gripping.

Amazing facts

- The Australian rocket frog covers an average of 25 body lengths in a single leap.

- The African pig-nosed frog does not use its legs to burrow. It uses its pointed, strong nose to dig holes.

- When attacked, the common toad swells up in size by gulping air and stands on tiptoe to make itself look much larger than it really is.

Climbing trees

Tree frogs are well **adapted** to living in trees. They have thin bodies with extra-long hind limbs. Their toes end in sticky pads that help them to grip the branches, especially when they are wet. They have good eyesight and can leap from branch to branch. Some even glide. They have large webbed areas between their toes, which can be used as a parachute to slow their fall as they leap from tree to tree.

Burrowing

Many frogs and toads make small burrows in which they hide during the day. Frogs living in an extreme environment may stay in their burrow for many months to avoid hot or cold weather. Frogs usually burrow backwards. They press their heels on the ground and push back and to the side, to sweep away the soil. This means that the frog's head is facing forwards all the time and it can watch out for predators.

Parental care

Most frogs and toads lay large numbers of eggs, but do not look after their eggs or their **tadpoles**. Only a few eggs and tadpoles survive to adulthood. The rest are eaten by **predators** or die from disease.

Some frogs protect their eggs so that they are not eaten before they hatch. One way is to keep the eggs out of water, which means they cannot be eaten by fish and other **aquatic** animals. Some tree frogs build nests of foam. For example, the foam-nest frogs of southern Africa gather on tree branches above pools of water to **breed**. When they breed, the female produces a **secretion**, which the males whip up into a foam using their legs. The female lays her eggs in the foam, which hardens on the outside but remains soft on the inside to protect the eggs. When the tadpoles hatch, the foam dissolves and they fall into the water below.

Amazing facts

- The Australian gastric brooding frog swallows her eggs and they develop in her stomach. She vomits up the tadpoles. These amazing frogs are so rare that they have not been seen since 1985 and may be **extinct.**
- The female mountain marsupial frog has pouches on her back in which her young develop. The developing young are joined to the mother's blood system so that she can supply them with food.

▼ The male olive midwife toad carries the eggs around with him for several weeks, keeping them moist by regularly visiting ponds.

Caring for their eggs

Many tree frogs lay their eggs in the tiny pools of water trapped in the leaves of plants. The female visits the pools of the tadpoles after they have hatched and lays unfertilized eggs, upon which they can feed.

Some frogs and toads carry their eggs around with them. The midwife toad lays strings of large eggs, which are **fertilized** by the male. The male then wraps these strings around his legs and carries them around with him. When the eggs are ready to hatch, he returns to a pool of water and releases the tadpoles. Other **species** carry their eggs on their back or in special pouches. For example, the female Surinam toad has special pockets on her back and the male places an egg in each pocket. The young grow inside these pockets and emerge as miniature frogs.

Darwin's frogs have an unusual way of looking after their eggs. These frogs are mouth brooders. The male takes the eggs into his vocal sac under his mouth. The eggs hatch and the tadpoles remain in the vocal sac. The sac gets steadily larger as the tadpoles grow. They stay inside the vocal sac until they are small **froglets** and can be released.

▲ Many **tropical** frogs produce a foam nest in which to lay their eggs.

► Tiny toadlets are emerging from pockets on the back of this female Surinam toad.

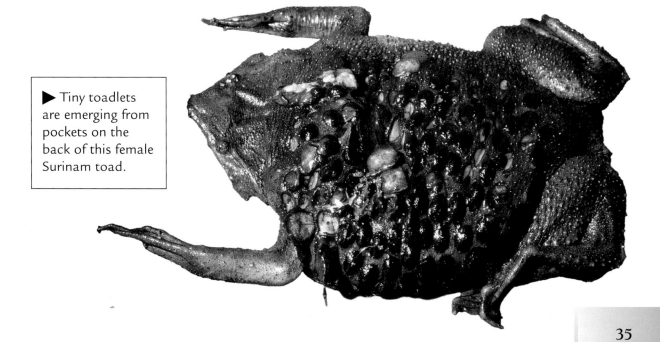

Poison frogs

Poison frogs are found in the rainforests of Central and South America. These frogs are from about 1.2 to 6 centimetres long. They **secrete** poison from their skin. Sometimes they are called poison arrow or poison dart frogs.

Poison frogs are very colourful, ranging from striking yellow and bright red to deep blue, orange and green. Some have spots or flecks, others stripes or swirls. These bright colours warn other animals that the frog is poisonous and not safe to eat. Poison frogs are not eaten by many other animals, but they will eat almost any insect that comes close.

Classification key

CLASS	Amphibia
ORDER	Anura
FAMILY	Dendrobatidae
GENUS	*Dendrobates*
SPECIES	about 170

Poisons

The different **species** of poison frogs have slightly different poisons, some of which are more harmful than others. People of the rainforest have long used the poisons from these frogs to put on the tips of their arrows. When the arrow punctures the skin of an animal, the poison enters their bloodstream and causes **paralysis**.

Poison frog life cycle

The blue poison frog has an interesting courtship. First, the male and female play by jumping around, chasing and wrestling with each other. Then, the female lays her eggs in water and the male **fertilizes** them. After the eggs hatch, the male takes care of the **tadpoles** until they are old enough to look after themselves. It takes about three months for a blue poison tadpole to **metamorphose** into a frog.

Some other poison frogs lay their eggs on leaves. About four days later the eggs begin to hatch and the tadpoles swim up the male's legs on to his back. He takes them to a safe pool where they are released into the water.

▲ The bright colour of the blue poison frog is a clear warning to other animals that this frog is very poisonous.

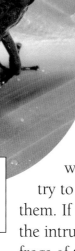

▲ This male poison frog is carrying one of his tadpoles to water.

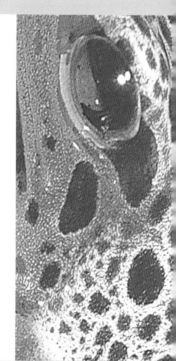

Fighting intruders

Both male and female poison frogs protect their **territory**, or space on the forest floor, against frogs of the same and other species. They can be quite aggressive. First they call out a warning. If this does not work, they try to scare away intruders by chasing them. If all else fails they fight or wrestle the intruder. Fights usually occur between frogs of the same sex, but sometimes males and females wrestle with one another.

▼ The golden poison frog is one of the most poisonous frogs.

Amazing facts

- The most lethal frog poison comes from the Koikoi poison frog of Colombia. Just 0.00001 grams is enough to kill an adult human.

- Sometimes a male tricks a female into laying eggs and instead of fertilizing them, he takes the eggs to feed to his own tadpoles.

Amphibians under threat

Amphibians around the world are under threat. There are many reasons for the decline in amphibian numbers and most are environmental.

Polluted habitats

One of the main causes of the loss of amphibians is destruction of their habitats by people. For example, streams, rivers and lakes are polluted by chemicals from industry, sewage from homes and pesticides from agriculture. Amphibians living in these polluted waters are unable to survive.

There are many reports of deformed frogs, for example, in 1995 a number of frogs with deformed back legs were found in Minnesota, USA. Similarly deformed frogs have been found in Canada and the UK. The reasons are uncertain but it could be linked with the use of pesticides or the result of an infection by a **parasite**.

Another reason for the decline in amphibians could be the loss of ozone in the atmosphere. Ozone filters out the harmful ultraviolet light in sunlight. Over the years, certain chemicals have been breaking down the ozone in Earth's atmosphere and this means that more ultraviolet light reaches Earth's surface. Ultraviolet light can damage the skin of people and cause skin cancers. The eggs and **larvae** of amphibians are also harmed by too much ultraviolet light, which causes them to develop abnormally.

▼ Ponds are essential for frogs and toads, but unless they are looked after they soon fill with mud and silt.

▲ The golden-striped salamander of Spain and Portugal is classed as endangered.

Spreading disease

Amphibians around the world, especially frogs, are being attacked by a disease caused by parasitic fungi. The fungus invades their skin and eventually kills them. There have been dramatic declines in numbers of amphibians in Central America, Australia and the western USA. Fungal spores are easily spread by animals and by humans who pick up the spores on their clothes.

Amazing facts

- During the last twenty years at least ten species of amphibian have become **extinct** in Australia, New Zealand and the surrounding islands.
- Worldwide, 91 species of amphibian are extinct, missing or critically endangered and a further 193 species are considered endangered or vulnerable.

Alien species

Sometimes amphibians are threatened by other **species** that are introduced into the habitat. They would not occur naturally.

These 'alien' species are often larger amphibians that compete with the **native** species for food and space. For example, in the UK many people bought non-native American bullfrog **tadpoles** for their ponds. Many adult bullfrogs have escaped, or people have released them into the wild, where they compete with native species. A similar problem exists in North America. The red-legged frog of the Pacific coast was once very common, but this species is also under threat from large bullfrogs.

▲ The golden toad was last seen in Monteverde cloud forest reserve, Costa Rica, in 1989 and is now probably extinct.

Protecting amphibians

One of the most important ways of saving **amphibians** is to look after their existing habitats and to establish new ones.

Many **species** of frog, toad and newt live happily in gardens and parks, so building wildlife ponds can help to provide new habitats. Ideally, the pond should have sloping sides so the amphibians can get into and out of the water. Frogs and toads are often called the gardener's friend because they eat many garden pests such as slugs. In farmland, ponds can be built in the corners of fields. A healthy amphibian population helps to keep down the numbers of insect pests.

Nature reserves

Important habitats for amphibians can be protected by making them into nature reserves. For example, the golden toad was very rare, so a reserve was set up in Monteverde, Costa Rica. Although these toads have not been seen for some time, the reserve protects many other species of amphibian. In the UK, the great crested newt and the natterjack toad are protected species and no one may collect or kill them. Their **breeding** sites are also protected.

Toad crossings

Each year, thousands of **migrating** frogs and toads are squashed on the roads as they return to breeding ponds. Many conservation groups have set up toad crossing patrols during the breeding season to carry the animals across the roads. Road signs can be placed near the ponds to warn motorists that there may be frogs and toads on the road. Some new road schemes have introduced amphibian tunnels so the animals can reach the ponds without crossing the road.

▲ In the UK, road signs warn drivers that toads may be crossing the road ahead.

▲ Toad tunnels allow toads to cross underneath major roads safely.

Amazing facts

- Plans have been made for 100 red-legged frogs, an endangered species living near the site of a new tunnel in California, to be moved to a new pond before the construction work begins in 2005.

- The skin of the White's tree frog has been found to have medicinal value. It **secretes** compounds that act against bacteria and viruses. It also produces a substance that has been used to treat high blood pressure in humans.

Toad barriers

The cane toad was introduced into Queensland in Australia to control some of the pests found in the sugar cane fields. Unfortunately, this large toad has bred so successfully that it has moved into habitats where it threatens the survival of **native** amphibians. Conservationists have built a barrier to stop cane toads spreading into northern Queensland, where they could threaten even more amphibians. Local people are encouraged to collect any cane toad that they find so that it can be destroyed.

▼ Cane toads are a major problem in Australia and barriers have been built to stop them spreading into conservation areas.

Classification

Scientists have found and classified about 2 million different types of animals. With so many **species** it is important that they are classified into groups. The groups show how living **organisms** are related by **evolution** and where they belong in the natural world. A scientist identifies an animal by looking at its features, for example, by counting the number of legs or what teeth it has. Animals that share the same **characteristics** belong to the same species. Species with similar characteristics are placed in the same genus. The genera are grouped together in families, families are grouped into orders and orders are grouped into classes. Classes are grouped together in phyla (singular:phylum) and finally, phyla are grouped into kingdoms. Kingdoms are the largest groups and are at the highest level. There are five kingdoms: monerans (bacteria), protists (single-celled organisms), fungi, plants and animals.

Naming an animal

Each species has a unique scientific name, usually called its Latin name, consisting of two words. The first word is the name of the genus to which the organism belongs and the second is the name of its species. For example, the Latin name of the common toad is *Bufo bufo* and that of the American toad is *Bufo americanus*. This tells us that these animals are grouped in the same genus but are different species. Many animals are given common names, but this may vary from one part of the world to another. For example, the frog *Rhinoderma darwinii* is called Darwin's frog, but it is also known by the name of the mouth-brooding frog.

For amphibians, a further grouping, the **super-family**, is used to show that a group of families have common features, but are not different enough from the other families to form a new order.

> ◀ Many tree frogs have several common names, so a unique Latin name is important.

This table shows how a common European frog is classified.

Classification	Example: common European frog	Features
Kingdom	Animalia	Frogs belong to the kingdom Animalia because they have many cells, need to eat food, and are formed from a **fertilized** egg.
Phylum	Chordata	An animal from the phylum Chordata has a strengthening rod called a notochord running down their back and **gill** pouches.
Sub-phylum	Vertebrata	Animals that have a backbone, belong to the sub-phylum Vertebrata. The backbone replaces the notochord.
Class	Amphibia	These are **vertebrates** that live in water and on land, with a smooth, moist skin.
Order	Anura	**Amphibians** with no tail and a short, rigid back with long hind legs belong to the order Anura.
Family	Ranidae	Frogs with long muscular legs, **streamlined** bodies and that lay eggs in water belong to the family Ranidae.
Genus	*Rana*	A genus is a group of species that are more closely related to one another than any group in the family. *Rana* refers to the genus.
Species	*temporalis*	A species is a grouping of individuals that **interbreed** successfully. The common European frog's species name is *Rana temporalis*.

Amphibian evolution

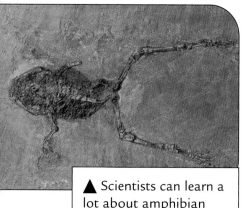

▲ Scientists can learn a lot about amphibian **evolution** from fossils. This frog fossil dates back to about 40 million years ago.

The development of **vertebrates** that lived on land started about 350 million years ago. At about this time, the climate of the world became hot and dry, causing the water in shallow pools and lakes to dry up. Some fish started to crawl out of the water and began breathing air.

Today, some fish can live out of water for long periods, such as eels, mudskippers and walking catfish. However, these fish do not have lungs or a strong fin structure to support their weight on land. The fish ancestors of the first land vertebrates must have had both these features. The most likely ancestors of **amphibians** were fish called crossopterygians, which were related to the coelacanth, a fish with fleshy fins.

First tetrapods

The earliest **fossil** tetrapods (vertebrates with four legs) were the Labyrinthodontia, large animals up to 1 metre long. A typical example was *Ichthyostega*. It was a cross between a fish and an amphibian. It had legs and could walk on land. It also had lungs, which meant it could breathe air.

About 250 million years ago, there were many different types of tetrapods. Many were smaller than the labyrinthodonts. Most of these tetrapods became **extinct**, but two groups survived. One **evolved** into amphibians and the other evolved into reptiles (see diagram page 45).

◀ Modern amphibians such as this toad are thought to have evolved from a group of ancestral amphibians called Lissamphibia.

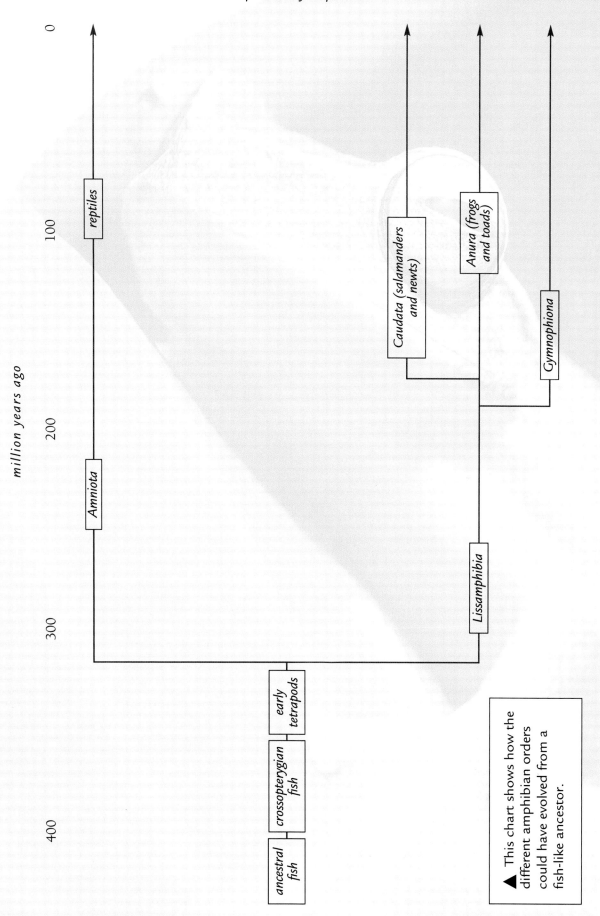

present-day amphibians

million years ago

0

100

200

300

400

reptiles

Amniota

Caudata (salamanders and newts)

Anura (frogs and toads)

Gymnophiona

Lissamphibia

early tetrapods

crossopterygian fish

ancestral fish

▲ This chart shows how the different amphibian orders could have evolved from a fish-like ancestor.

Glossary

adapt change in order to cope with the environment

algae simple, non-flowering plants found in water

amphibian animal that lives part of its life on land and part in water, though there are a few exceptions

aquatic living in water

blood vessels tiny tubes that transport blood around an animal's body

breed reproduce

caecilians worm-like amphibians

camouflage colouring that blends with the background, making an animal difficult to see

carnivore animal that eats other animals

characteristic feature or quality of an animal, for example having hair or having wings

clutch more than one egg laid by one female

dormant inactive

ectothermy having a body temperature that rises and falls with the outside temperature, often referred to as cold-blooded

embryo unborn or unhatched young

evolution slow process of change in living organisms so they can adapt to their environment

evolve change very slowly over a long period of time

extinct no longer in existence, to have permanently disappeared

fertilize cause a female to produce young (an egg or live young) through the introduction of male reproductive material

fossil remains, trace or impression of ancient life preserved in rock

froglet small, young frog that has just emerged from water and has lost or is losing its tail

frogspawn mass of frog's eggs

gill part of the body that an aquatic animal uses to collect oxygen from water

gland organ that releases a substance, such as saliva or sweat

herbivore animal that eats plants

interbreed mate with another individual of the same species

invertebrate animal that does not have a backbone

larva young animal that looks different from the adult and changes shape as it develops

mammal class of vertebrates that feed their young milk, are usually covered in hair and have a constant body temperature

mate reproduction partner of the opposite sex or ability of male to fertilize the eggs of a female of the same species

metamorphosis process of changing from one form to another during development. In amphibians it is usually associated with a change from an aquatic larval stage to a terrestrial adult stage.

migrating making a regular journey, often linked to the changes of the seasons

mucus slimy substance that is released by the skin of amphibians

native local to or born in an area

nocturnal active at night

northern hemisphere half of the Earth above the equator

nutrient substance that provides nourishment essential for life and growth

organism living being, such as an animal, plant or bacterium

paralysis condition in which the muscles cannot move

parasite animal that lives on or in another animal

pigment natural colouring of animals

predator animal that hunts other animals

prey animal that is hunted by another animal

reptile ectothermic, egg-laying vertebrate with tough skin covered in scales

secretion substance released from part of the body

southern hemisphere half of the Earth below the equator

species group of individuals that share many characteristics and which can interbreed to produce offspring

streamlined having a slim shape that moves through water as easily as possible

super-family group of families with similar features that are not different enough from other families to form a separate order

surface area total area of the outside of an organism or object

tadpole larval stage in the life cycle of a frog or toad

terrestrial living on land

territorial behaviour of an animal when it is defending its territory

territory range or area claimed by an animal or group of animals

torpor state of inactivity

tropics region of the world that lies either side of the Equator, with a hot, often wet climate

vertebrate animal that has a backbone

viviparous giving birth to live young

Further information

BOOKS TO READ

Burnie, David (Editor-in-chief.) *Animal – The Definitive Guide to the World's Wildlife* (Dorling Kindersley, 2001)

Clarke, Barry, *Eyewitness Amphibian* (Dorling Kindersley, 2002)

Fridell, Ron, *The Search for Poison-Dart Frogs* (Franklin Watts, 2002)

Halliday, Tim and Adler, Kraig, *The New Encyclopedia of Reptiles and Amphibians*, (Oxford University Press, 2002)

WEBSITES

http://www.bbc.co.uk/nature
A searchable website that gives news, statistics and photos of all animals, including amphibians from frogs to newts.

http://elib.cs.berkeley.edu/aw/amphibian/facts.html
AmphibiaWeb provides information on every recognized species of amphibian in the world. The website has species descriptions, life history information, conservation status, photos and range maps.

http://www.open.ac.uk/daptf/index.htm
The aim of the Declining Amphibian Populations Task Force (DAPTF) is to find out the nature, extent and causes of declines of amphibians throughout the world, and to promote means by which declines can be halted or reversed.

http://www.nationalgeographic.com/ngm/0105/feature6/index.html
Web pages devoted to frogs, with interesting articles and wonderful photos and links to other websites.

Index

Titles in the *Animal Kingdom* series include:

Hardback   1 844 43773 6

Hardback   1 844 43772 8

Hardback   1 844 43771 X

Hardback   1 844 43767 1

Hardback   1 844 43766 3

Hardback   1 844 43769 8

Hardback   1 844 43768 X

Hardback   1 844 43774 4

Find out about the other titles in this series on our website www.raintreepublishers.co.uk